Make Money Online

21 Proven Ways to Make EASY Part-time Money Working Online

Amanda Kline

Table of Contents

Bonus:

Free Video Reveals _How to Get_ _$1,000, $3,000 & $5,000 Commissions_ Deposited Directly Into Your Bank Account without Every Picking up the Phone

Watch Now - > http://bit.ly/1k-3k-5k

Disclaimer

This book has been written for information purposes only. Every effort has been made to make this book as complete and accurate as possible. However, there may be mistakes in typography or content. Also, this book provides information only up to the publishing date. Therefore, this book should be used as a guide - not as the ultimate source.

The purpose of this book is to educate. The author and the publisher do not warrant that the information contained in this book is fully complete and shall not be responsible for any errors or omissions. The author and publisher shall have neither liability nor responsibility to any person or entity with respect to any loss or damage caused or alleged to be caused directly or indirectly by this book.

Introduction

In this day and age there are thousands of ways to make money online, however, it doesn't mean that they are all created equal. Many people have succeeded, and many people have failed. Some people failed because of their lack of knowledge in the industry, or maybe they bought into a scam. But for the people who have succeeded, and will succeed, they followed the proven steps to make money online.

In this book, *Make Money Online- 21 Proven Ways to Make Easy Part-Time Money Working Online*, we are going to talk about exactly that- proven ways to make money online. It is my hope that after you finish the pages in this book you'll have a fire lit to go and make some money online!

Take note that the order I have listed the proven steps is not important. None is more important than the other. Many steps will obviously overlap and work together. Depending on where your strengths and weaknesses lie, you'll be able to pick and choose which steps you do yourself and which ones you'll need to outsource or get some help with. So read all the way through and get excited!

Just like any business venture, you don't have to be the smartest or the first on the scene. You need to be creative, diligent, and consistent. The World Wide Web (internet) is a vast resource, a blank canvas that you can write your own story upon. So let's get started with these 21 proven steps so you can learn how to make money online.

1. Make Money with Freelance Writing

If you have any writing skills at all this is one of the easiest ways to make money working online!

When you're a freelance artist that means people commission you to paint a specific painting for them. The same applies to freelance writing. People have articles, books, newspaper copy, magazine copy, etc... that need written and they either don't have the time or the talent to do it themselves. That's where you come in. Every job will obviously be different in its content and length. It will just depend on what the client is looking for.

Finding these job requests can be as simple as doing a Google search for "freelance writing". It will pull up multiple job requests, all yours for the taking. Of course, depending on how strong your writing skills are that will determine which jobs are for you and which are best left for someone else with a different writing skill level. I'll give you some actual websites later on in this chapter that are dedicated to writing job requests.

So get your wheels turning. As a freelance writer potential clients could literally be almost anything. Think of your everyday world and all that you see that is "written". Potential clients could be any small, medium or large business owner that has a website, bloggers who need help writing topic-specific article, online marketers, companies that own catalogs and need help writing clear, concise product descriptions. You get the point.

It's totally up to you and your personality in how you want to approach being a freelance writer. You can pick a niche and stay within its confines because that's where you feel comfortable and most knowledgeable, or you can apply for a variety of jobs and topics and learn as you go. Taking the "learn as you go" approach is definitely more interesting, but it will slow down your process (because you'll be doing more research to catch up to speed on a topic/concept you're not as familiar with). I think this is a more valuable approach to your craft because it will stretch you and cause you to do some extra learning. Neither approach is wrong. Just pick what works for you.

A very important component of making money online with freelance writing is gaining a working knowledge (or brushing up) of keyword research. Your Google, Bing, Yahoo, etc… are the powerhouses of getting people to the places they want to go online. There are countless websites and many times they are in competition. Think of a category like "sporting goods". There are so many massive retail chains and smaller businesses all competing in the same arena. These search engines evaluate websites (and their pages) by analyzing their keywords for type, frequency, and distribution.

Many times, as a freelance writer, your job will require that you properly apply keywords to your work. You'll need to do your keyword research for the topic and allocate those keywords as evenly as possible throughout the article.

As you get started in freelance writing, there are two ways to conduct your business. First, you can write articles on particular topics and then sell them in bundles. You'll need to do your research in niches to see what people are going to want articles written on, but think 3,100-word articles on "how to use things in your kitchen to make non-toxic household cleaners", or "how to integrate email campaigns into your business to boost profits". Then once you know what people need written material on you'll need to know where to go to advertise your articles.

If that doesn't interest you, or at least not right now, the other approach is to seek out the jobs that you find posted online. You can respond to as many job postings as you feel comfortable. This will definitely take a little more time because you'll need to scroll through multiple sites to research these jobs and communicate with the client, but it will help give you actual topic direction on your writing.

Here are some recommended freelance sites:

www.elance.com

www.odesk.com

www.needanarticle.com

www.iwriter.com

www.fiverr.com

www.microworkers.com

2. Make Money on Fiverr.com (Very easy)

What if you could get paid $5 over and over again for doing something as easy as a voiceover or posting on Facebook? You can! It's almost too good to be true but at www.Fiverr.com you can sell any service you want for just $5.

You can get paid for all the usual serious stuff or some pretty hilarious things!

Here are some of the more serious categories

- Help with SEO
- Creating video testimonials
- Writing articles
- Doing voiceover work
- Transcription
- Song mixing
- Foreign language translation and more!

Now if you want to hear some of the things a little more on the crazy side…here you go. These are some actual listings on Fiverr

- I will write your message on my big belly and dance in the jungle
- I will prank call anyone anytime anywhere
- I will sing happy birthday as tin foil man wearing just a thong
- I will promote your business with a lighted pumpkin

- I will write you message in the sand on a Jamaican beach
- I will video chat with you
- I will act and talk like a pirate and say anything you want on video
- And more…

If you want to check out more gigs like this just check out the "fun & bizarre" section of Fiverr.com

3. Make Money as a Virtual Assistant

Virtual assistants are becoming more and more popular!

The internet has made it easy for someone to hire and virtual assistant without feeling like they are virtual.

Virtual assistants do all kinds of jobs. Here are some sample activities:

- Online shopping
- Research
- Writing
- Setting appointments
- Computer work
- Making travel arrangements
- Order gifts
- And more…

Your boss' imagination is the only limit really.

Here are some great websites to get hired as a virtual assistant.

www.Odesk.com

www.Elance.com

www.VirtualCoWorker.com

www.Zirtual.com

Just as in any job your pay can range depending on who are working for and what your skills are.

4. Make Money Giving Away Gift Cards

All businesses need leads. Many companies are willing to give away huge gift cards just to get an email address. They are also willing to pay you for helping them get that lead!

Let me give you an example. One company I know gives away a $100 Victoria's Secret gift card just for some entering their email on their website. So you wanted to make money with this offer you would get a specific website link that is tracked to you that you could post on your Facebook, Twitter, Instagram, or any other form of telling people about this offer.

Each offer comes with a specific website link that is tracked to you so you know how much money you are owed! Pretty fun way to make money huh?

The $100 Victoria's Secret gift card is just one sample. There are many other offers like:

- Best Buy gift cards
- Free x-box gift cards
- Free gas gift cards
- Wal-Mart gift cards
- And much more…

Here are some great websites to find these types of offers:

www.NeverBlue.com

www.MaxBounty.com

www.ClickBooth.com

5. Make Money with Affiliate Marketing

Affiliate marketing is where you promote and advertise someone else's products and/or services for them, not as the seller, but as an affiliate. That means you earn a commission off of the sale, not the entire sale. So the seller who wants others to promote their product or service (thus to increase exposure and in turn sales) will normally have affiliate specific links that track any sales the affiliate makes so that commission credit can be given out appropriately.

While affiliate marketing is definitely easier to do, it may take a little time to build up an income. The pros are that you don't have to fulfill anything. You don't have to ship a product. You don't have to email an eBook, audio, or video. You just help promote and cash in a commission from the seller. But as previously mentioned, you're definitely going to need a lot of traffic to hit your affiliate link to build up your income.

One approach to affiliate marketing is to promote someone else's product alongside your own. Let's say you're a personal trainer and you have a great list and following. Maybe you have a great nutrition info product that you're promoting (it's yours) and then also as a great addition you have an affiliate link for your favorite "best abs" book. You can promote both yourself and someone else's product to add value for your customers, but you'll also add money to your bottom line.

The most well-known and number one affiliate network for digital products is called Clickbank (www.clickbank.com) You can get an account for free and start searching which products you'd like to promote and begin earning commissions from. You can also add your information products to this site and have people sell your products for you as well.

Other great websites to find affiliate products are:

www.JVzoo.com

www.CJ.com

www.Amazon.com

www.NeverBlue.com

www.MaxBounty.com

Bonus:

Free Video Reveals *How to Get $1,000, $3,000 & $5,000 Commissions* Deposited Directly Into Your Bank Account without Every Picking up the Phone

Watch Now - > **http://bit.ly/1k-3k-5k**

There are plenty more affiliate platforms but those are some of the best with high paying programs

6. Make Money "Tweeting" on Twitter

Advertising is a big game and people pay big bucks for it. The trouble with most advertising is that people know its advertising!

But when you see a social media post from a friend, people tend to trust it a lot more. That is where the opportunity comes in for you. Business's are now "paying per tweet" for you to send out a specific message! Pretty good idea huh?

You can make really easy money doing this. Generally the business gives you exactly what they want you to "tweet" and when to "tweet" it. All you have to do is schedule it.

To get connected with advertisers that are paying per tweet just go to one of the following websites:

www.PaidPerTweet.com
www.SponsoredTweets.com
www.Paid2Twitter.com

Of course you can do your own research and find more.

7. Make Money with Youtube.com

Ever been on youtube and seen those little ads that pop up either before the video or during the video? Yea the owner of those videos is making money every time you see one of those ads! That could be you!

The key is to coming up with topics that people want to watch.

A couple of the vest types of videos to start with are:

- Educational videos
- Product reviews

Because you can start with something you are very familiar with. Say its "protein powder" you might start by doing a video review each day on different types of proteins.

When you enable YouTube ads you have the opportunity to make money every time someone sees that video!

Now as far as making the videos you can either record yourself or you can do more of a screen capture video.

If you want to do the screen capture videos here are some great resources:

Windows Movie Maker- usually comes installed on most PC's

Camtasia – www.techsmith.com

Jing - http://www.techsmith.com/jing.htm

Screenflow (Mac) – www.screenflow.com

8. Make Money Hosting Interviews

This is a pretty simple way to make money online. Simply interview someone and then, either:

- Sell the interview

- Post it on your blog (which has ads on it to make money from)
- Or Post it on YouTube (which also has ads to make money from)

Now, obviously it has to be someone that people want to hear from. It can't be Aunt Martha's dog walker. Clearly, no one will buy, or at least not many.

What's the deal with interviews? Why would someone want to buy one? We are in an information hungry age, and people want to know straight from the horse's mouth how/why/what/when etc... Or sometimes it's just flat out juicy details and gossip that sell. So there's always that route too.

As the interviewer, you're free to conduct your interview the way you see fit. However, the most common ways are your traditional Q&A

format or more laid back approach of having a series of questions to ask them but allowing the interviewee to talk and ask more questions as the conversation flows. The latter approach is a little more natural. Either is acceptable. It will just be a preference for either you or the interviewee. Q&A can seem a little more boring and rigid, but if a time frame is strict then this format will help keep you on point. Q&A can be a good place to start, and then as you're confidence and comfort level grows you can switch to the more questions-based approach.

Make sure before each interview that you talk with your interviewee and gather their preferences when it comes to questions. There may be some things that are off limits for them, or they may be open to the whole gamut.

Once the interview is scheduled it's really up to you if you want to sell it as a transcript, an audio recording, a video, or all of the above.

9. Make Money from Your Hobbies

Is there a hobby in your life that creates a physical product? Maybe you love to create artwork. You should sell them online. You can definitely sell them on a local level via sites such as Craigslist.org; however, there's a much bigger world out there that may be interested in your product. So why not capitalize on that and try to sell it on a broader scale?

Your product(s) to sell could be anything. Only you know what you're skilled at and what you enjoy producing. It could be simple knotted bracelets, knitted hats, or grandiose paintings. One of the fastest growing platforms for people to sell their creative works is Etsy. You could have an Etsy store up and online by the end of today. It's a phenomenal digital marketplace for all things handmade. If you haven't visited Etsy.com before go check it out!

As previously mentioned Craigslist is a place to advertise your products (not the best but you might as well not leave it out). Also, EBay or your own website or blog are other great places to advertise your creative handiwork.

Things that are handmade can always garner a higher price because it was made by hand, has attention to detail, and people know it took that person a substantial amount of time, creativity, and a little bit of their heart and soul. So enjoy your work, be proud of it, and go sell it!

Here are 3 great places to sell your own products:

www.Etsy.com

www.Ebay.com

www.Ebay.com

…And let's not forget selling on your own website! Here's my favorite platform for building a great e-commerce store and selling your own products.

www.Shopify.com

10. Make Money Selling Stock Photos

It seems that everyone instantly became a "photographer" with the introduction of affordable great-quality digital cameras. That's not a bad thing for you. It opens up the market and makes it so much easier to capture scenes in our world. Even all of our smart phones today have better cameras than any of us had as kids growing up. Making money by selling stock photos does not mean you'll be entering these photos into contests or trying to sell prints online (which, of course, you could always try if you want). It means you'll be uploading them to stock photo sites where people can them purchase them to use them for personal or business purposes.

Stock photography is the production of photograph for paid or even free usage. A customer will purchase your photo and pay a one-time fee. They will then own the rights to use the photo at their discretion, wherever they choose and however many times. It's not a pay-per-use business model.

But if photography is something you have an eye for and you're skilled in capturing moments, images, objects, monuments, scenes, human interactions etc… then this is a great way to make money online. Or even if you love to travel, simply documenting your travels (monuments, historic sites, beautiful vistas, children in the streets, the hustle and bustle of a colorful market etc…) could be a way for you to earn an income as you travel.

But if travel isn't your thing, then the general idea of stock photography is to think about what people would need a picture of. The options are truly endless. So ideally you'll want to pick a niche, something that interests you. Let's pick a popular niche- health and fitness. There's a high demand for health and fitness-related photos for personal trainers, gym owners, fitness equipment business, etc… to use on their marketing materials and/or website. You could photograph a person smiling drinking their protein shake, someone lifting weights, weights carefully placed on the gym floor, someone in a yoga flow, someone drinking their refreshing water post-workout, and on and on. You get the point!

Maybe that isn't your niche. Maybe you love people and capturing elements of human emotion. So you could capture photos that portray happiness, joy, sadness, or frustration. Anything that someone can then take and use on their site to help convey their message. Someone that looks frazzled sitting at their desk with a pile of papers could portray a variety of things. It could be someone who is overworked or someone who needs help with their organizational skills. If someone has a business service that helps people get organized they might utilize this photo.

Stock photography is still your creative work so you can set parameters on it if you choose to. The general mode of operation for most stock photographers is to sell it to the customer for a one-time fee with unlimited usage. If you choose to you can place limitations on how many times it's used or the time period for which it is valid for usage. The most important thing to remember is to properly assign those rights to your stock photos.

A few really great stock photo sites…

www.istockphoto.com
www.bigstockphoto.com
www.dollarphotoclub.com

11. Make Money Blogging

Being a blogger can make you money online in and of itself, but if you combine affiliate marketing and even selling your own products, you'll only increase your profits. If you love to write and share information then this will be right up your alley.

A "blog" (or web log) by definition is an online record of your activities, life, and anything else you want to share. You may want to take the avenue of a personal or community blog where you speak on topics that are important to you. If that's the case then making money online with that type of blog will look a little different. Perhaps you add a "donation" section on your site where you accept donation for a cause or charity that you're passionate about. So if you're passionate about organic farming and all that entails, you may find a 501c3 organization that supports organic farmers and their families. You may be pleasantly surprised at people's generosity.

But if you're interested in a blog that is selling and promoting products and services, this will be where more of the moneymaking potential lies. Your blog is your affiliate marketing link canvas. You can write about your passions and sell things related to it, or simply just use it as a business platform. So start writing and creating interest content for the world to see, start building your blog following, and start incorporating products and services to sell (affiliate links) that coincide with the mission of your blog.

As a side note, always be careful with your personal and business information. Nothing about a blog is "private". Just like anything that goes out into cyberspace... it stays there.

A few recommended blogging platforms...

Wordpress (hosted) – www.wordpress.com
Wordpress (self-hosted) – www.wordpress.org
Blogger – www.blogger.com

12. Making Money Managing a Blog

Just like almost anything, there will always be people who want to have "something" but they don't want to or don't have the time to dedicate to the task. Blogs are beneficial to many businesses. Sometimes that is your sole business- your blog. Creating and maintaining a rocking blog that's not only compelling, interesting, and profitable is not rocket science, but it does take time. It takes time to update, create new things, and maintain it. Like we mentioned early, many people want to have a great profiting blog but they don't have the time or don't want to dedicate the time to it. That's where a blog manager comes into play.

I mentioned Wordpress in various chapters prior to this one, but it is one of the most common for blogging. It's a software program that allows you to write and publish your blog with a lot of automation built in. You can get it to auto-respond for you, monitor your stats (i.e. how many visitors) etc…, but this all requires the use of the different available plug-ins. These plug-ins are actually small portions of code that tell the site to perform a specific task.

All that to say, there are tons of plug-ins and many of them don't "play" well together. So you need to choose and manage these plug-ins well to keep your blog in tip-top-shape! Depending on the client that has hired you as a blog manager will determine your actual tasks as manager. You may be asked to contribute as a write, link up all the appropriate affiliate links from their writing contribution, manage and update plug-ins, post the blogs, etc... It's an awesome convenient service that you can provide as a blog manager. It will be up to you and the client's needs to determine what you'll charge for the project.

If you're not familiar with Wordpress and all of its various plug-ins, now would be the time to do that. You may even want to gather some of your favorite plug-ins and settings to use as a template for when you take on each new blog management client. Blog management is all about helping blog owners with the problems they encounter and getting paid for it.

13. Make Money with Audio/Video Transcription

Many people need audio or video transcribed. You can take audio and video and transcribe them into text format. This could be anything from a "how to eat better for fat-loss" video that someone wants to basically turn into an eBook, or transcribing audio or video pieces for the hearing impaired.

It could simply be a written transcript of the audio or video file in a Microsoft Word or PDF format, or even adding the subtitles to the video format for an enhanced experience.

You can transcribe your own material to create additional products, or like we've discussed a few times in this book about making money online, you can offer your transcribing services on any of the job posting sites online. It's a bit of a tedious task so most people will want to hire out for it instead of doing it themselves. It's tedious but rather simple. You'll just need to have rather decent typing skills or else the project most likely won't be worth your time.

Post your listing on www.Fiverr.com for the best results on this.

14. Make Money on Craiglist.org

www.Craigslist.org is huge! You probably already know that. But what you may not have thought of is that many people have things they would love to sell on craigslist but don't have the time to do it.

Why not find those people and charge them a percentage of the sale price to sell their stuff for them?

This is very easy to do! You can start by talking with your friends and family, ask for referrals, post on social media, or even run ads about your new service.

Yes this takes some work but it can very lucrative.

15. Make Money with Graphic Design

Do you have any basic, or even experienced, level of skill utilizing Photoshop or any other image editing software? Maybe you learned how to use it in school, and you've just used it to edit your personal photos. It's quite an enviable skill to have. So if you have it great. You're primed to be able to make some money online with that skill. Even if you don't have the aptitude at Photoshop or other image editing software, but you're eager to learn, you should definitely dedicate the time to learn. Keep in mind you do need to have a natural talent base of graphic style. You need to have an "eye" for what looks good. That skill can be honed, but you definitely need to have some spacial-awareness to know what looks good as it's presented on a page.

The good news you do not have to be a Photoshop master pro extraordinaire to make money online. Graphic design can encompass a wide range of projects: anything from cropping or editing photos, resizing images, or creating a project completely from scratch, for example maybe a book cover design or a company's new logo.

If you haven't dipped your toe into the world of graphic design, start small and start your pricing accordingly. As you build your portfolio of art and projects you'll be able to charge more money as you gain more confidence and increase your skill level. So if you're the "creative" type this will definitely be right up your ally! The Internet is a vast world, and there is plenty of graphic work to be done.

Just like doing research for keywords is super important for making money online with your writing skills, doing your research in the graphic design world is equally important. Begin to research companies' logos, newsletter layouts, postcards, etc… Start to take note of popular trends and what works well in particular settings. For example, something for a medical-related business or article wouldn't want some design that's completely crazy and outside the box. It would be a little cleaner, more streamlined look. Just start your research and what matches up with your current talent level.

Another idea to get your work "out there" is to submit your work to various art websites such as deviantArt. Make sure to be up to date on all copyright and intellectual property rules so that you stay on the straight and narrow. You may unintentionally use a background for your original piece that someone else created. That can definitely get you in trouble even if it's unintentional.

There is nothing wrong with utilizing images that you didn't create yourself. Artists do this all the time. They incorporate an image from someone else into their creative design. The key is making sure that it's a royalty-free image. Either you paid to have the right to use it or the artist has it out there for free. Plus, just as you wouldn't want to take someone else's work as your own, you don't want the same thing happening to you. So do your homework and get informed on how to protect your images!

A great website to check out for cheap royalty-free stock photography is…
https://DollarPhotoClub.com

Social media is here to stay, and thus it creates a market for all sorts of custom design work on people's personal and business pages. Think Twitter, Facebook, & Instagram. Many people want backgrounds or "meme" images created for their personal or business pages.

The Warrior Forum is fantastic site to offer your graphic design services. You may also want to check out fiverr.com where you can apply for or list a variety of design jobs.

Sites to check out…

http://fiverr.com

http://www.warriorforum.com/warriors-hire/

16. Make Money with Logo & Design Contests

Who doesn't love some healthy competition, right? The demand for updating a company's "look" or logo will always be high. People want to stay on the cutting edge and be fresh. So there are plenty of opportunities out there for logo design and general design.

So you definitely need to the technical skills and talent to pull this off, but if this is your forte then it can be a great way to make money online. You'll compete with a variety of artists for the same project. This means you'll be given the general idea and constraints of the project from the client, and then you perform with your creative skills.

This is obviously subjective work. The client may love your work or they may choose someone else's. These contests, however, do give you great practice in your skill set and help you build your portfolio.

As a reminder, when you enter a contest make sure and read everything the client proposes. They could be extremely picky and specific, or they want to let your creativity reign. So make sure and get your ducks in a row before you get started.

A few recommended sites (two mentioned in the previous chapter)...

http://www.warriorforum.com/warriors-hire

http://fiverr.com

17. Make Money Building Wordpress Sites (Easier than you think)

In this day and age it's basically a requirement that if you own a business you need a website. The general public's expectations of website design are high. If people encounter issues accessing your site, or it's not user-friendly and very confusing, many times they'll give up. Most likely you'll have lost the sale or at least the potential sale. So needless to say, a good first impression on a business website is just as important as an in-person impression.

You may be thinking to yourself, "I don't know how to code things. I'm not a web-specialist. I have no clue how to make a website." So that's either you, or maybe you have a little working coding knowledge. Good news for both of you. With the advent of platforms such as WordPress, they have leveled the playing field for many in website design. There will definitely be a learning curve just to get familiar with WordPress and how to set up a site, but with this tool you truly can create a great, semi-customizable site for yourself or a client.

Unless you were a web-designer in a former life *(which if you are, what a fantastic skill set to have…put it to use!! You obviously don't need this chapter)* get to work and start doing your homework. Web-design has both a huge creative and practicality component to it. So you'll need to utilize both your left and right brain. You'll need to think beauty and function simultaneously.

Great communication with your client will be of utmost importance so that you can properly portray their vision onto the pages of their site. But with WordPress you truly can offer someone a great site that can be updated with relative ease, for a decent price. Not that you're not worth charging higher prices…that will come. You'll be able to tackle more projects using a platform like WordPress and earn great money online because you're not building a website from complete scratch.

So dig in and get to know WordPress (or other platforms like it) so you can start making money online. You can post your web design services online, on facebook, or any other place you would normal offer your business services.

You can find plenty of pre-built themes at sites like: http://themeforest.net

18. Make Money Dropshipping

If you like the idea of buying at whole and selling at retail but you don't want to worry about spending a bunch of money on inventory then dropshipping may be your game.

There are many suppliers that are willing to provide you with a list of their products for you to advertise on your website then once an order has been placed they will ship the order from their warehouse. You pay them for the wholesale price and keep the difference.

This is a great way to test whether or not a certain type of product will sell well. Once you sales volume gets big enough you can start to look at other options like buying wholesale, where you will have more overhead but also make a bigger margin.

Dropshippers are generally pretty easy to find. Just do a Google search for "Dropshippers + {your product niche}. For example, you might search "dropshippers + stuffed animals" to get started in that niche.

19. Make Money Wholesaling

The most common type of individual business that you will find online is one that sells products direct to the consumer. Just like a brick and mortar store buys products from suppliers and then re-sells them, you can absolutely do the same thing online!

Let me share an example. A great friend of mine owns two fitness studios where we live and this studio requires that you wear a particular kind of sock for the optimal workout, as the workout requires that you do not wear shoes, just this particular sock. So my friend, let's call her Katie, decided to start her own sock company so she could not only make money off of the memberships at her studios, but also from the socks that people need for the workouts. Now, of course, you can wear "regular" socks to this workout, but the ones she sells are optimal because they have little grips on the bottom that make your workout more effective. So she buys these socks from a supplier at a bulk discount, uploads pictures and item descriptions on her website, and marks up the price of the socks to turn a profit.

She's got a perfect system where the marketing is pretty much built in. All the people at her studios have a demand for these socks. However, to really increase her business she will need to spend money and effort in her marketing to expand her market. This is just one example of how to sell other people's products to make money online.

Your biggest task will be in choosing your products that you will sell. It needs to be a niche that you have researched well, and that you know there is demand for. You'll need to research suppliers and find the suppliers that will make the most sense for your business. Not only will bottom line cost be important and making sure there is enough margin to actually make a profit, but also transit and shipping times will come into play. If you have a supplier that has a 3 week lag time on delivering their products to you, that is definitely something you have to always keep in mind. You'll have to be on top of your inventory and make sure you're not going to run out before the next delivery!

Again, advertising is always going to be a major player in this game of making money online. They say, "you're not in business until people know you exist and desire your product." You can have the best product in the world, but if no one knows who you are and that you exist it doesn't matter. You'll need to employ a marketing strategy, either that you have created or that you have recruited someone else to help you with. You may choose to advertise with Facebook ads, pay-per-click, pay-per-view, banner ads etc...

Since this is in online venture you obviously need a website. This does not have to be the most extravagant site you've ever seen. Too many people get caught up in that. There are times where that's necessary, but the really important components are that your site is "clean" looking (not jumbled and overloaded with too much "fluff"), organized, and easy to navigate. It should be explicitly clear where to go to shop and purchase your products. After all, that's what you want people to do- shop and buy your stuff.

Make sure on your site you have a protected checkout system so that customers' credit card data is secure. You can use easy platforms such as Paypal, Shopify, Woo Commerce etc... to help build out your store on your site. Plus, don't forget you'll need space for your product inventory. That's the offline part of your business. So designate a space and get organized there before orders start to come in.

20. Make Money with Your e-book

The world of information products has exploded in the past few years. If you're not familiar with what an information product is, you've encountered many of them without knowing it. It's any item, in this case in text form, that was created by someone to fulfill a need or that customers may find value in.

The easiest, and most common, type of product to create is an electronic book, aka eBook. You'll be writing on a topic you have great knowledge on or one that you've researched well because there's a great demand for that information. As easy as that...You have an info product.

You can get started with your eBook as simply as opening up Microsoft Word or another program like it and adding those words to the pages. You can also get a free version called OpenOffice at www.openoffice.org

Maybe it's a book you want to create. Or maybe it's just a "how-to-guide". The sky really is the limit, you just need to have a good idea of what people will actually want to purchase. The easiest part is creating your product and making it look aesthetically pleasing. The hardest part is selling it.

So your biggest challenge will be in the promotion of your product. There's always going to be competition, but you need to have the knowledge or hire someone with the knowledge to get your product the right exposure it needs to sell.

As a general rule when you're writing your info product, it needs to be substantial. Not just the length of an average article. People are not going to spend their hard earned money on a few hundred words. You're definitely going to want to aim for a few thousand words to have a product that's worthy of charging a price.

You may decide it's not an eBook that you want to write, but maybe a full-course on how to do something, or a package that includes information, graphics, charts, etc... Whatever it is... get to writing!

Don't forget about the very important component of writing- editing. If this is not your forte then find someone who can do it well for you. Editing is crucial and will only add to the value of your product. You want to do everything with excellence, as it ultimately is a reflection of you.

After all this talk about writing a book or info product, in theory it sounds great, but the idea of actually doing it makes you want to vomit. That's totally understandable. We all have different strengths. But let's say you have some really great concepts that you'd like to focus an info product(s) around. Good news! Just like with almost anything, you can hire someone to write it and/or design it for you.

A couple great sites to post a job to are...
www.elance.com
www.odesk.com
www.fiverr.com

You'll post the job with all the details of your info product, and then different people will apply for your job. Then you can read through their application/portfolio to see if they are the kind of writer you'd want to hire.

After someone completes your info product for you, you have the choice to sell the product under your name or use a pen name. It really is up to you and your business strategy. However, if you do use your name and someone else wrote it for you, be extra diligent that it "sounds like you". Not someone else.

So choose your niche(s) and start the creation process so that you can make money online with your info product!

As a side note, once you've created your product via Microsoft Word, or something like it, it's best to convert your file to PDF so that it's a little more protected.

Once you have you product made you will need a place to sell your product. For that I have a few suggestions.

www.Clickbank.com

www.Amazon.com

www.JVzoo.com

21. Make Money with Your Own Audio Book

The world of audio is growing. People want to be able to multi-task and listen to something while doing something else. Enter audio products.

There are a few routes to take with audio products. First, you can use your text-based info product and re-create it in audio form. Now you have two products to sell instead of one. Secondly, you can audio record other people's products. Maybe it's an eBook written by someone else or paper that needs audibly dictated. Lastly, you can just create a new audio only product. Audio is a powerful from of communication and one that is in demand in this day and age.

Audio info products are great for the person who has a long commute, or it may just be their preferred learning style. So that just means yet another market for you to make money online!

There's a great free program that you can get started recording with today. It's called Audacity.

You can download the software here...
http://audacity.sourceforge.net/

If you've never done any audio recordings then it is definitely time to start practicing. You can play with your voice to find the optimal sound, which will of course depend on the project. But to get started just play around recording different things. You'll be able to edit out any dead air moments or "umm's and ahh's".

You'll need to do some self-criticism and make sure that your words are annunciated clearly, that you don't slur anything that you speak clearly and concisely, etc... It'd be great to have a close friend listen to it as well to give you some honest feedback. Then once you've worked on your audio recording skills you can get to work making money online!

Check out all the previous listed sites to look for audio recording job postings and also http://acx.com for jobs to record audio books.

Concluding Remarks

I hope you've enjoyed learning about how to make money online. The online marketplace really is vast. There are so many opportunities to make money online. It's just like any career- you need to evaluate your strengths and talents and then choose how you'd best like to make money online.

Make sure to take advantage of the websites and resources listed in this eBook to help you in your journey. If you enjoyed reading this book and found it valuable, I would love it if you would give me a 5 Star Rating and review on Amazon.com!

To your success,

Amanda Kline